THE INNER WORK OF WORK

COACHING YOURSELF FOR IMPROVED PERFORMANCE

GETTING ALONG WITH OTHERS

MICHAEL BAROFF

BK

BERRETT-KOEHLER COMMUNICATIONS, INC.

Berrett-Koehler Communications, Inc.
450 Sansome Street, Suite 1200
San Francisco, CA 94111
Phone: 415-288-0260
Fax: 415-362-2512

ORDERING INFORMATION

Please send orders to Berrett-Koehler Communications, P.O. Box 565, Williston, VT 05495. Or place your order by calling 800-929-2929, faxing 802-864-7626, or visiting www.bkconnection.com.

Special discounts are available on quantity purchases.
For details, call 800-929-2929.

Printed in the United States of America on acid-free recycled paper.

ISBN 1-58376-154-3

CONTENTS

Welcome to the Inner Work of Work

You have in your hands a guidebook for dealing with some of the most common issues you will face in the workplace. As you explore these issues you will embark on a journey that will expand and deepen your relationship to the realities of work and, most assuredly, give you an advantage in a changing and competitive job market.

In this guidebook, I present prevailing human resource development, training, and organizational development ideas in a simple and direct manner. The intent is to give you access to and an enhanced personal understanding of the factors executives and managers encounter in trying to improve a company's performance through the efforts of the people like you who work in that company.

The material is written in a format that will enable you to think about, reflect on, and come up with your own perspectives and solutions. This approach is the essence of "inner work."

Though it appears to be simple and direct, doing inner work will require your focus and attention if you are to stretch beyond your current capabilities. With this understanding, I trust you will come to appreciate the value of not only reading but also working through the material. As you use this guidebook, appreciate that you will gain confidence both through the process of developing your own insights and from the specific results you achieve by acting on those insights.

Let's look for a moment at the connection between inner work and improved performance. While on the job, your focus and attention are, by and large, on creating tangible bottom-line results, products, services, revenue, and profit. You strive to produce something of value or get things done in a timely and cost-effective manner. You attend meetings, plan, organize, and perform tasks and activities to achieve results. Of course, all this is what work is externally about, but what is behind or underneath all this activity?

The focus on inner work puts the responsibility on you to reflect on, then stretch beyond your usual approach and come up with responses to essential work issues such as the following: What motivates me to succeed? What do I need to learn in order to develop and grow? Where I am going in my career? How can I communicate more effectively, so that I am understood? How do I deal with conflicts? Where do I fit into the big picture? How can I take a leadership role? What is the meaning or purpose in what I do? Whom am I serving by the work I do? Am I manifesting my creativity? Am I experiencing joy in what I do?

Some of these questions may seem a bit philosophical for typical work-related conversation, but they are the essence of what inner work is about. Inner work is about becoming aware of the qualities, capabilities, and attributes you bring to what you do and creating a sense of personal meaning and commitment from that awareness.

Ask yourself where you are on the following continuum in your relationship to your work:

1. Are you just showing up in order to survive?
2. Are you interested and engaged in what you do?
3. Are you willing and able to push beyond your limits and boundaries?
4. Are you fully committed to achieving and succeeding with purpose, meaning, and a clear sense of inner direction and personal satisfaction?

By doing inner work you can shift your perceptions and working relationships to improve your performance by coming to terms with what serves or doesn't serve you, those you work with, and the company you work for, and then deciding what to do about it.

You may ask yourself why it is so important to take time to think about and reflect on workplace issues. Consider what has been going on in workplaces over the past few years. There is widespread and deep change in expectations about work and the social contract between employers and employees. To compete in the global marketplace, employers are restructuring their businesses, reorganizing departments and functions, reengineering work processes, and redeploying people. There is also an emerging perspective that employees are no longer simply "human resources," but rather are "human capital," whose value is a function of the productivity they create for the organization that employs them. These dynamics are neither good nor bad; they are just the way it currently is. Although any guarantee of lifelong employment in any one company is nearly gone in all industries, including the government sector, there is also an emerging expectation on the part of employers that employees be accountable for their performance and that employees be stakeholders in the results they produce. Employers are looking to recruit and retain the best employees, who are able to take responsibility for their own job development and performance improvement.

From an employee's point of view, another set of expectations is emerging about quality of personal, professional, and spiritual life. You spend a large portion of your daily life in the pursuit of and the doing of work, and the workplace can provide you with much of the grist for not only job and career development but also personal development. As the nature of work has evolved from purely industrial to "knowledge-based" your individual and our collective effectiveness and productivity have come to depend less on the sweat of our physical labor than on the essence of our being. Thus, it is also your spirit that may now desire to be nurtured.

This guidebook, *Getting Along with Others*, addresses the *behavior and skills* that enhance communication and relationships with other people. You will examine how your behavior is perceived by others, learn how to develop trust, enhance how you listen and develop rapport when communicating, set the stage for dealing with differences and conflict, and present yourself assertively when working with others.

You may find value in the other guidebooks in this series:

Contributing to Your Company's Success addresses the *organizational dynamics* that create and support a productive work environment. This guidebook gives you the tools to determine where you fit into a company's big picture. You will learn how to work as part of a team, understand how a company evaluates the bottom line, determine how to add value in what you do, and develop your own approach to being a leader.

Being Your Best addresses the *attitudes* of personal success that are determined by self-awareness and the choices you make. This guidebook will enable you to come to terms with who you are, what you have to offer, and where you want to go in your work life. You will explore your beliefs about work, what motivates you to succeed, how to use your creativity and intuition, tap into your energy and feelings, clarify the roles you play at work, learn how to adapt to change, and create the outcomes and lifestyle you want.

As you read through each guidebook and explore the issues connected to your work-related personal, professional, and spiritual growth, I invite you to consider the following overarching question:

How can I approach my work life as an ongoing quest to maintain awareness of my inner mental, emotional, and essential processes while coming to terms with what in my experience nurtures me and what I must move through or beyond in order to change or improve my on-the-job performance?

The guidebooks provide you with a road map to refer to as you embark on this journey of performance improvement. You are the one in the driver's seat, choosing the milestones you want to reach, how slow or fast to go, and when and where to make a turn or take a rest.

What Does It Mean to Coach Yourself?

When you think about the role of a coach, you are likely to imagine someone who works with a sports team or an individual athlete. Some people who work out at a local gym use a personal trainer or coach to help keep them on a schedule and a regimen for cardiovascular, aerobic, and weight training in order to trim down, tone up, and develop strength. The goal of coaching is to improve performance. Interestingly, people who use coaches tend to be those who are already motivated and committed to improving and thus attaining the highest performance possible for themselves.

In the workplace, it is typically executives who engage the services of a coach. One would think that executives would already have achieved success and high performance. However, as with the athletes and teams who use a coach, it is those on the path of development who are aware of their own limits, yet know they could do better if given a little assistance from someone who has their interests and goals in mind.

Viewed from a larger perspective, coaching focuses on helping you achieve three overall goals:

- To become responsible for your own ongoing development
- To achieve and maintain productive interpersonal relationships
- To commit to achieving organizational goals through improved performance

To achieve these goals, it is important for you to clarify and appreciate the value you offer through the work you do, develop ongoing and supportive ways of communicating with your co-workers, and continually focus on how your performance affects organizational goals.

Let's explore the dynamics of a coaching relationship. The qualities of a coach include being trustworthy, open and honest, sincere, committed, and nonjudgmental. A coach asks questions, challenges, listens, pays attention, and stays focused on the acknowledged purpose. It is important for you to incorporate the qualities of a coach into your own mindset. By learning to coach yourself, you will be able to make changes or improvements in your attitude about your work, your behavior at work, your ongoing job, your career or professional development, your performance and achievements, and your personal sense of success.

Ultimately, the effort you must make comes down to doing an "inside out" job. That is, you—not your manager, supervisor, teacher, trainer, or coach—have to make the change or improvement. Likewise, who else but you could know, determine, or care most about your path of growth and the pace at which you move along that path?

Who but you has the most capacity to listen to what you think and feel? I firmly believe that the answers to your work-related questions and challenges are within you.

What might it mean for you to learn how to coach yourself? At first the idea may seem like a contradiction or an oxymoron. I don't mean to suggest that this process should be done entirely alone or in isolation from what is going on where you work. Rather, I believe it is important to create a climate and expectations for integrating your inner work into your day-to-day work-performance improvement efforts.

With this belief in mind, I have developed what I call "Coaching Points." These Coaching Points are analogous to the coaching points someone playing a sport or doing a personal fitness program would work on to improve performance. For instance, a tennis player might practice specific components of the game such as the serve, forehand, backhand, and mental focus in order to improve overall performance. Someone on a health and fitness program might work on diet, endurance, muscle strength, and flexibility in order to enhance well-being. In either situation, the coaching process involves structured practice on a series of integrated exercises to achieve an overall goal.

This guidebook is designed to walk you through a series of "Coaching Points" that will help you gain deeper insight and ability to directly address your on-the-job situations. In the process, you will learn how to coach yourself for improved performance.

Why Get Along with Others?

***Getting Along with Others* helps you take advantage** of the unique opportunity you have to interact with the diverse range of people you work with, people you might never have otherwise met through your friendships, families, and community. The workplace, on a daily basis, forces us to interact and negotiate with people who have a range of personal styles and competencies. We also must confront our and other's prejudices and biases and resolve conflicts of communication and perspective. All of this challenges us to maintain our integrity while collaborating and teaming with others. The *Getting Along with Others* guidebook is your interpersonal relationship coach.

As the economy has grown over the past decade, approximately 12 million new workers have entered the workforce. Workforce demographics show increasing numbers of people of diverse ethnic and racial backgrounds, recent immigrants, women, and younger workers who may lack basic job skills, as well as older workers who are deferring retirement and remaining on the job.

In my consulting practice, I have interviewed members of work groups in order to understand what's going on between people and enhance team work. I have heard people tell the most passionately detailed stories about grievances or breaches of trust that have kept people from talking with each other. Invariably, when I ask when the offense occurred, I learn that the event occurred years ago, though it is still talked about as if it had happened that morning. Then, during a meeting to mediate the issue, the parties come to realize that the whole scenario was based on a simple misunderstanding. How much time, energy, and productivity has been lost?

Communicating directly and clearly is a challenge for most of us, especially when we are placed in the stressful situations that often occur at work. When situations get tough we often rely on defense mechanisms that distance us or put the blame on others. We protect ourselves by thinking or saying things like, "It's all their fault;" "If it weren't for such and such, everything would work better," or "No one understands me." While there may be elements of reality in such statements or there may be a precipitating event, the growth-oriented work is looking within ourselves to determine our own role in the communication gap.

Are you involved in a disagreement or conflict with someone at work? Perhaps you have had a falling out with someone in the past that has resulted in a strained ongoing working relationship. Have you found yourself avoiding or not knowing how to connect or talk with someone? By taking yourself through the Coaching Points in this guidebook you will explore, for instance, how to give feedback to people about how their behavior affects you, how to avoid pushing others' "hot buttons," how to listen and show empathy, how to develop rapport using different styles of communication, how to address levels of conflict, and how to assert yourself in order to get your needs and wants met.

This guidebook will help you do the inner work necessary to become aware of your own perceptions, thoughts, and feelings, and how they affect the interactions you have with other people.

Getting Started

This guidebook is comprised of a series of what I call "Coaching Points," each focusing on an area that influences how people commonly approach work. You will find a Coaching Point on, for example, behavior, another on trust, and so on. There are 20 Coaching Points in all and each one takes you step by step through a process of thinking about and reflecting on an area that has direct impact on your work. Each Coaching Point concludes by asking you to develop an action plan based on what you have learned during the process.

Below I give a brief introduction to the Coaching Point concept and its various parts, explaining how a Coaching Point is designed and giving you some ideas about how to work through them.

First, notice that each Coaching Point is formatted to contain the following elements:

- A *Definition* defines or describes a main idea or concept.
- A *Simple Truth* expresses the essential meaning underlying the Coaching Point.
- *For Your Consideration* presents a probing question, thought, or example that reinforces the practical implications of the Coaching Point.
- A sequence of *First Steps* offers ways you can begin to explore the Coaching Point. Some steps suggest things to think about now or things to do when certain situations arise.
- A *Reflection* prompts you to rely on your own inner guidance in thinking more deeply about the Coaching Point and applying it.
- The *Next Step* encourages you to take immediate action to follow up and implement the Coaching Point.

The sequence in which each of these elements is presented is designed to allow you to explore, unfold, integrate, and apply the learning associated with each Coaching Point. The process will support you in coming up with your own insights and actions.

It will be helpful to have a writing pad, notebook, or journal at hand in which to write down your thoughts, responses, and insights as you go through the material.

Before you begin, select a comfortable and quiet place to read and work through the material. Allow yourself a minimum of 15 minutes to work through each Coaching Point.

If you don't have the time or don't feel the need to go through the material in a structured manner, you can rely on the guidebook as a desk reference or on-the-job performance aid. Keep the guidebook visible on your bookcase as a handy resource to reinforce essential expectations about your on-the-job performance. You can always pick up the guidebook, begin anywhere, follow your inclinations, and trust that you will learn what you need when you need it.

To help you get the most out of doing the inner work presented in this book, I walk you through a sample Coaching Point. In this walk through (which follows) I do two things. First, I offer some suggestions for how to approach each element of the Coaching Point. I refer to these suggestions as "Coaching Prompts." Second, I share some brief excerpts of my own thoughts and reflections that are taken from my personal self-coaching work. I label these responses "Thoughts." My purpose here is to model what inner work *can* look like, not what it *should* look like. I encourage you to find your own, unique approach to doing inner work.

Before you embark on your own inner work, let me leave you with this thought. Doing inner work is not always easy, but neither is it complicated. It simply involves taking the time to step back from the automatic, quick, and often hurried reactions you may have to issues and situations before you take action. Inner work allows you to take on the role of observer in order to become more aware of both your thoughts and how they are translated into action. In cultivating your ability to act as a reflective observer of your own thinking you become your own coach—a coach who is honest, sincere, committed, and nonjudgmental, who listens and asks probing questions, and who can be trusted to keep your best interests and purposes in mind.

Congratulations! You are about to begin a journey of self-awareness and development that will serve you throughout your work life.

■ *Coaching Point Walk Through* ■

BEHAVIOR is the *conduct* people display that affects how others respond to them—either positively or negatively.

> SIMPLE TRUTH
>
> *Behavior, not personality, can be changed.*

Coaching Prompt ➤ As you read the statements, consider what stands out for you in the wording of the description or definition. Does the Simple Truth ring true for you? If so, recall a situation in your personal experience that makes it real for you. If not, what situation in your personal experience suggests a different way to interpret the statement?

Thoughts ✍ Does my behavior differ from my personality? People often tell me I seem to be easygoing. I know that when I get really focused on what I'm doing I can get stressed out and be abrupt and critical of people.

Recalling that recent stressful project makes me question how people interpret my different behaviors. I know that I get impatient at times if things aren't going how and when I expect them to go.

➧ FOR YOUR CONSIDERATION

People will be more open to change when their behavior is pointed out to them in a way that maintains their self-respect and affords them the opportunity to suggest how they can improve rather than being told what to do.

Coaching Prompt ➤ Think about the practical implications and consequences of the For Your Consideration statement. Again, recall a personal experience that either reinforces the message of the statement for you or suggests a different perspective. Remember, the statements are only guides; it is your experience that is real for you.

Thoughts ✍ I really hate it when John says, "What I think you should do is . . . " or "Here's the right way to do it." It makes me feel like an idiot, especially when in front of the rest of the group. I know I resisted doing what he said for a day or so.

FIRST STEPS

To initiate change in someone's behavior:

1. Describe the behavior to the person. "When you . . ."
2. Say how that behavior makes you feel. "I feel . . . " (for example, "angry," "sad," "hurt")
3. Express why the behavior affects you in that way. "Because I don't feel . . . " (for example, "heard," "appreciated," "respected")
4. Ask for suggestions for ways to change. "Do you have any suggestions for how to change things the next time this situation comes up?"
5. Listen to the other person's viewpoint and continue to talk about the situation from your own point of view.

Coaching Prompt ➤ Read through each of the First Steps and make some notes to yourself in response to the questions or suggestions. Perhaps there are specific resources or information in your workplace that can help you move through each step.

Thoughts ✍ I know I get upset when people are late for a meeting or don't deliver what they promised on time. I really feel disrespected. Sometimes I just hold in my frustration, and it can affect my whole day. I guess I can let them know this is how I feel when they're late.

REFLECTION

Consider how your own behavior has contributed to someone else's behavior.

Coaching Prompt ➤ Before you explore the Reflection, take a deep breath and get into a relaxed and open state of mind. Then read the statement and take a few minutes to look within yourself to explore any meaning or significance the statement has for you.

Thoughts ✍ Now that I recall, when John got on my case that day, it was when I was already irritated about something else and wasn't really participating much during the meeting that day.

NEXT STEP

Consider someone whose behavior in a particular situation you want to change. Outline the sequence for giving feedback for this situation. Provide them feedback in the next appropriate situation

Coaching Prompt ➤ You should now be ready to outline some Next Step actions. Be very specific when you write down each action. Make an agreement with yourself as to when, where, and with whom to follow up with action. Appreciate and acknowledge your progress no matter what pace you move at on your journey.

Thoughts ✍ That being late really does bother me. I can just say, "Sarah, I know we are both under pressure, but when you're late to our meeting, I feel that you don't respect my time. I would appreciate it if you would let me know you're going to be late so I don't have to stop what I'm doing."

COACHING SESSION ONE

Examining Your Behavior and Perceptions

In this session you will explore the following Coaching Points:

- BEHAVIOR
- ASSUMPTIONS
- VULNERABILITIES
- TRUST
- HELP

The foundation for getting along with others is your ability to examine your behavior and appreciate how that behavior is perceived by others. Likewise, it is important to become aware of the assumptions that you, knowingly or unknowingly, have about people and situations in order to prevent misunderstandings and foster open and honest communication.

Becoming sensitive to your own as well as other people's basic human vulnerability enhances your capacity to develop and maintain trust, which is a keystone for all positive interaction. All of these factors contribute to the ease with which you will be able to develop mutually helpful, supportive, and productive working relationships.

BEHAVIOR is the *conduct* people display that affects how others respond to them—either positively or negatively.

> SIMPLE TRUTH
>
> *Behavior, not personality, can be changed.*

FOR YOUR CONSIDERATION

People will be more open to change when their behavior is pointed out to them in a way that maintains their self-respect and affords them the opportunity to suggest how they can improve rather than being told what to do.

FIRST STEPS

To initiate communication about someone's behavior:

1. Describe your perception of the behavior to the person. "When you . . ." (for example, ignore me, raise your voice, make a joke)
2. Say how that behavior makes you feel. "I feel . . . " (for example, "angry," "sad," "hurt")
3. Express why the behavior affects you in that way. "Because I don't feel . . . " (for example, "heard," "appreciated," "respected")
4. Ask for their suggestions for ways to change. "Do you have any suggestions for how to change things the next time this situation comes up?"
5. Listen to the other person's viewpoint and continue to talk about the situation from your own point of view.

REFLECTION

When was the last time someone told you what to do? How did you feel at the time? Did you do what they wanted? Why or why not?

NEXT STEP

Consider someone at work whose behavior in a particular situation affects you. Outline the sequence for giving feedback on this situation. Take the opportunity to discuss this feedback with them.

ASSUMPTIONS are the private thoughts and feelings you take for granted, which form the basis for your view of people and situations.

> SIMPLE TRUTH
>
> *When you identify and express an assumption you have about someone or something, you begin the process of letting it go.*

FOR YOUR CONSIDERATION

Assuming that only you know what or who it takes to get a particular job done the "right" way can lead to misunderstanding or conflict with others.

FIRST STEPS

Consider the following ways that assumptions affect communication:

1. *Confiding* occurs when there is sharing of an assumption with someone else.
2. *Misunderstanding* can occur when people keep their assumptions hidden from each other.
3. *Blunders* can occur when someone is unaware of the effect their assumptions about someone else have when made apparent to another person.
4. Open *communication* occurs when each person is aware of both his or her own and another's assumptions and is willing to explore their similarities and differences.

REFLECTION

What is an assumption you feel someone else has about you? How has this perception affected your communication with that person? What is an assumption you hold about someone or some situation at work? What prevents you from expressing or testing the reality of this assumption openly?

NEXT STEP

Arrange an appropriate time and place to discuss how an unexpressed assumption you have made about someone at work has led to a misunderstanding.

VULNERABILITIES are *"hot buttons,"* which, when pushed, can wound someone's sense of personal power and obstruct effective communication.

> SIMPLE TRUTH
>
> *Being able to exploit someone else's vulnerability may allow you a quick win, but it will destroy an ongoing relationship.*

FOR YOUR CONSIDERATION

Personal wishes or demands to be treated fairly and equitably are often based on having had a vulnerability exploited.

FIRST STEPS

When dealing with sensitive situations:

1. Be aware of warning signals in yourself or others, such as the following:
   - Body reactions such as muscle tightness, a twitch, or skin flush
   - An uncomfortable silence in the conversation
   - An outburst of nervous laughter
2. Acknowledge to others that you are aware of the warning signal or discomfort.
3. Imagine how the other person is feeling.
4. Ask people to comment on their own experience of what is happening.

REFLECTION

Recall a time recently when you lost control of yourself at work. What words, behaviors, or issues pushed your buttons? How did this reaction affect communication with the other person?

NEXT STEP

Describe your personal warning signals. What can you do to regain your composure when you feel pushed?

TRUST is the willingness to *rely* on the best intentions of someone else.

> SIMPLE TRUTH
>
> *Trust, once lost, may take a long time to regain, or it may never be regained.*

FOR YOUR CONSIDERATION

A climate of trust supports people to be and grow into who they are, release the fear of retaliation and punishment, appreciate how they are interdependent, and optimize the process of working together.

FIRST STEPS

To build and maintain trust:

1. Be open and honest with information.
2. Commit time and energy to relationships.
3. Follow up on agreements.
4. Listen to and respect other points of view.
5. Share recognition with others.
6. Invite and accept feedback.

REFLECTION

Recall a work situation in which your trust in someone was violated. What were the circumstances? How did the situation affect the ongoing relationship? Were you able to regain trust, and if so, what did it take?

NEXT STEP

Describe specific things you could do to inspire the trust of your co-workers.

HELP is the *assistance* or *support* everyone needs every so often to get unstuck.

> SIMPLE TRUTH
>
> *The best way to help people is to help them figure out their own solutions.*

FOR YOUR CONSIDERATION

Develop a network of mutual support by getting together at breaks or lunches with others to casually chat about what's on each of your minds.

FIRST STEPS

1. Offer help with an attitude of *service*, or wait until asked.
2. *Communicate* in order to offer help in a supportive manner:
   - Encourage ("Tell me about . . . ")
   - Clarify ("When did this happen?")
   - Summarize ("Let me see if I understand the situation:")
   - Acknowledge ("I can see that you are upset . . . ")
   - Solicit ("I would like your opinion about . . . ")
   - Respond ("I see it this way. . . . How do you see it?")
   - Empathize ("I appreciate why you feel that way.")
   - Reflect ("It looks/sounds/feels like . . . ")
3. *Avoid* creating roadblocks to offering help:
   - Ordering ("You must . . . ")
   - Threatening (If you don't, then . . . ")
   - Preaching ("You should . . . ")
   - Lecturing ("Don't you realize . . . ")
   - Giving answers ("If I were you, I'd . . . ")
   - Judging (You're just being . . . ")
   - Prying or cross examining ("Why?" "How?")

REFLECTION

Recall a situation when you helped someone. How did the per son show appreciation? Recall a situation when someone helped you. How did you show your appreciation?

NEXT STEP

Describe a few work-related situations in which you could use some help. List who you could ask for that help in those situations.

SESSION SYNTHESIS

- What insights or new awareness did you gain in this session?
- What key learnings are associated with those insights?
- Which Coaching Points or aspects were easier to work through?
- Which Coaching Points or aspects were more difficult to work through?
- What specific steps or actions have you already taken? What occurred or didn't occur?
- What specific steps or actions do you feel most resistant to taking? What is underlying that resistance?
- What questions or concerns remain unanswered for you right now? What are you going to do about it?

COACHING SESSION TWO

■

Enhancing Communication

In this session you will explore the following Coaching Points:

- LISTENING
- OPENNESS
- RAPPORT
- STYLES
- EMPATHY

Now that you have examined some of the underlying aspects of your behavior, the next component of *Getting Along with Others* develops your ability to clearly and directly communicate and connect with other people.

All work involves communication in some form or fashion. Given that each of us has had different life experiences, perceives those experiences with a unique set of personal characteristics, and may communicate those experiences with a style different from that of others, it becomes essential to take the time and effort to demonstrate that you understand where others are coming from.

The essential ingredients for enhancing communication are listening to and being open and honest with others, developing an interpersonal rapport based on appreciation of each person's unique style of communication, and showing concern and empathy for others as they, like you, strive to be understood.

LISTENING is the process of *receiving* messages (ideas, questions, feelings) from another person.

> SIMPLE TRUTH
>
> *Words convey only a small amount of any message; much of what is communicated is nonverbal.*

FOR YOUR CONSIDERATION

Be sensitive to the difference between acknowledging that you understand and agreeing to what someone says.

FIRST STEPS

To actively listen to another person

1. Be alert to how they communicate:
   - Eyes
   - Facial expression
   - Body language
   - Speech patterns (volume, tone, and timbre)
   - Spoken words
2. Maintain a mutually comfortable posture and distance from the other person.
3. Open your mind and heart to the other person by letting them know and feel that you:
   - Hear what they are saying
   - Understand how they perceive circumstances
   - Appreciate who they are right now
   - Are truly interested and concerned
   - Have no desire or need to change, judge, or evaluate them

REFLECTION

The next time you are talking with someone at work, notice whether you are preparing what you want to say to them while they are still talking.

NEXT STEP

Describe ways in which you could improve your listening skills.

OPENNESS is the ability to *appropriately share*, confide, or disclose personal information to others in order to develop intimacy and trust.

SIMPLE TRUTH

Treat friends as friends, family as family, and co-workers as co-workers.

FOR YOUR CONSIDERATION

How comfortable is it for you to talk to someone at work about a work-related success? A work-related mistake? What you did over the weekend or on vacation? How a situation at home is affecting your day?

FIRST STEPS

Before sharing personal information with others at work, ask yourself the following questions:

1. Will it add to an ongoing work relationship?
2. Is there an opportunity for the other person to also share?
3. Is your timing in the here and now?
4. Is the setting mutually comfortable?
5. Is there a reasonable risk involved?

REFLECTION

What issues or topics determine your boundary between appropriate and inappropriate personal sharing in the workplace? Do others know your boundaries? How might you convey your boundaries if you feel that someone has stepped over the line? Do you have different boundaries for different people that you work with? What are they?

NEXT STEP

Describe what you could share with whom in order to develop a closer working relationship.

RAPPORT is *connecting* and *relating* with another person by being aware of how your way of communicating affects them.

SIMPLE TRUTH

Rapport in the workplace should create warmth and understanding, not heat and seduction.

FOR YOUR CONSIDERATION

Perceptions of inappropriate behavior or harassment often occur when a conscious expectation or an unconscious desire to create rapport crosses the other person's line of propriety.

FIRST STEPS

To develop rapport with another person:

1. Try to speak with similar vocal characteristics to the other person:
   - Volume (soft/loud)
   - Tone (high/low)
   - Pace (slow/fast)
2. Try to breathe at the same rate as the other person.
3. Adjust your body posture and movements to reflect those of the other person.

REFLECTION

What communication characteristics do you share with your best friend that contribute to your getting along? How are those characteristics different from those when you relate to people at work?

NEXT STEP

Describe ways in which you could create a positive rapport with a particular person at work.

STYLES are the ways people prefer to communicate with others.

SIMPLE TRUTH

The more you can match another person's style, the better your interpersonal communication and rapport will be with that person.

FOR YOUR CONSIDERATION

People perceive information, relate to others, and interpret reality through a combination of senses.

FIRST STEPS

Become aware of people's preferred style and respond appropriately:

1. Notice the wording the person uses to perceive; do they process information predominantly through their visual, auditory, or tactile senses?

If they say, for example:	Then respond by, for example:
• "I *see* what you are saying."	Writing ideas on paper, showing charts and pictures.
• "I *hear* your concern"	Changing your tone, volume, pitch, and rate of speech to emphasize points.
• "I *feel* your anxiety."	Creating a comfortable environment before talking about an issue.

2. Notice whether the person relates more thoughtfully, emotionally, or physically:
   - If more thoughtful, then respond with a logical argument and facts.
   - If more emotional, then respond by telling descriptive stories.
   - If more physical, then involve them in doing activities.

3. Be sensitive to whether they have a more casual and spontaneous manner or a more formal and traditional manner.
4. Distinguish whether the communication is oriented toward being more content- and task-oriented or more relationship- and process-oriented.
5. When communicating with a group of people, it is helpful to mix communication modes in your presentation:
   - Include pictures, verbal descriptions, and movement.
   - Present ideas, examples, and experiences.
   - Match your manner to the dominant styles in the group.
   - Focus on process to achieve task.

REFLECTION

Describe characteristics of your preferred style. How does your preferred style match the style of particular people you work with?

NEXT STEP

Practice using a variety of styles when you communicate.

EMPATHY is demonstrating to another person that you *understand* and *care* about what is important to them.

SIMPLE TRUTH

You don't always need to do something; sometimes it's enough to just be there *and* pay *attention.*

FOR YOUR CONSIDERATION

Saying something like "I appreciate why you feel that way" shows respect without being judgmental and opens the door to sharing your own feelings.

FIRST STEPS

To enhance communication and demonstrate your empathy with someone else:

1. Appreciate that *everyone*, regardless of their personal and cultural values and beliefs, has a need for:
   - Physical security
   - Social interaction
   - Self-esteem
   - Self-actualization
   - Spiritual connection
2. *Develop* rapport, comfort, and trust with others so that you can talk about what may be affecting your working relationship.
3. *Listen* openly with your heart and mind to the other person's thoughts and feelings.
4. *Respond* by acknowledging, both verbally and nonverbally, the feelings the other person expressed.

REFLECTION

Recall a situation when someone at work completely and deeply understood you. What did the person do to communicate understanding? How did you feel at the time? How do you feel about that person today?

NEXT STEP

Describe a situation at work in which you could demonstrate more empathy.

SESSION SYNTHESIS

- What insights or new awareness did you gain in this session?
- What key learnings are associated with those insights?
- Which Coaching Points or aspects were easier to work through?
- Which Coaching Points or aspects were more difficult to work through?
- What specific steps or actions have you already taken? What occurred or didn't occur?
- What specific steps or actions do you feel most resistant to taking? What is underlying that resistance?
- What questions or concerns remain unanswered for you right now? What are you going to do about it?

COACHING SESSION THREE

■

Dealing with Differences

In this session you will explore the following Coaching Points:

- GUIDELINES
- RESPECT
- CONFLICT
- QUESTIONING
- UNDERSTANDING

Though you may do your best to examine your own behavior and perceptions and build rapport and trust with others, inevitably the inherent differences we each demonstrate may contribute to misunderstandings. Thus, a very significant aspect of getting along with others is your ability to confront and productively deal with everyday workplace differences.

Dealing with differences initially involves setting guidelines for how to most appropriately interact with others. As you have already explored, we each have a wide range of unique personal and professional knowledge and experience, so it is extremely important to acknowledge the value that each person brings to any situation. However, you must also be prepared to approach these potentially differing and conflicting perspectives with an open mind and focus on asking questions in order to develop clarity and mutual understanding.

GUIDELINES are the basic understandings for engaging in a productive interpersonal or group activity or meeting.

SIMPLE TRUTH

People resent wasting time and energy in unproductive meetings.

FOR YOUR CONSIDERATION

Most workplace interactions are opportunities for people to:

- Solve problems
- Plan actions
- Share information
- Provide feedback

FIRST STEPS

When interacting with others one on one or in a meeting:

1. Stay focused, listen, and participate.
2. Make statements, then invite questions.
3. Agree on what important words mean.
4. Give reasons behind your statements, questions, and actions.
5. Focus on interests, not positions.
6. Respect people's need for confidentiality about sensitive issues.

REFLECTION

Recall a time when you left a meeting totally energized and ready to take action. What occurred during the meeting that contributed to your feeling?

NEXT STEP

Outline suggestions for improving your next meeting.

RESPECT derives from *appreciating* that every person interprets experiences through their own *filters* of *reality*.

SIMPLE TRUTH

You do not have to totally understand someone else's reality in order to work with them.

FOR YOUR CONSIDERATION

Filters of individual reality include:

- Age
- Gender
- Culture, race, and ethnicity
- Sexual/affectional orientation
- Socioeconomic status
- Social, political, religious, and spiritual affiliation
- Attitudes, prejudices, beliefs, values, and opinions
- Interests and experiences

FIRST STEPS

To enhance mutual self-esteem, belonging, and respect:

1. *Ask* people to share their experiences and perspectives.
2. *Share* your experiences and perspectives.
3. *Explore* similarities and differences with an expectation of building on your respective uniqueness.
4. *Engage* others by finding out how they want to be treated.

REFLECTION

Describe the attributes of people you most easily get along with. Describe the attributes of people you have more difficulty getting along with.

NEXT STEP

Describe the attributes associated with your own filters or reality.

CONFLICT occurs when people *disagree* over: (a) facts; (b) methods for getting something done; (c) the goal or reason for doing something; and/or (d) the underlying assumptions, values, and beliefs each person holds.

It is easier to resolve (a) than (b), (b) than (c), and (c) than (d).

> **SIMPLE TRUTH**
>
> *Conflict can be an opportunity for creative problem solving.*

FOR YOUR CONSIDERATION

The most creative solutions seek to address everyone's needs. Less satisfying is to compromise, split the difference, accommodate someone else, neglect your own interests, agree to disagree, or avoid discussing the issue altogether.

FIRST STEPS

To confront a work conflict:

1. Focus on the *issue*, not on someone's personality.
2. Explore what each person has an *interest* in achieving.
3. Come up with some *options* that might benefit each person.
4. Agree on *how* and *when* the issue will be resolved.

REFLECTION

Consider a conflict you have had with someone at work. What might have been an issue or conflict you had within yourself that you may have attributed or projected onto the other person?

NEXT STEP

Describe some creative ways to approach a work-related issue or conflict you are dealing with.

QUESTIONING is a basic way to *learn* how other people experience situations.

> SIMPLE TRUTH
>
> *Intelligence is often demonstrated by the questions you ask rather than the answers you give.*

FOR YOUR CONSIDERATION

Some people feel comfortable jumping into a discussion to offer their thoughts, while others prefer to be invited to share their perspective.

FIRST STEPS

To explore a situation or issue, ask questions in the following sequence:

1. Ask about what people objectively *saw* or *heard*.
2. Ask them how they *feel* about the situation or issue.
3. Probe to find out what it *means* to them.
4. Ask what their next step, decision, or *action* might be.

REFLECTION

Whose perspective is most often heard in your work group? Whose perspective is often missing?

NEXT STEP

Draft some questions to help discover the missing perspective.

UNDERSTANDING is being able to acknowledge a point of view different from your own.

SIMPLE TRUTH

By listening before you speak,
you can prevent misunderstanding.

FOR YOUR CONSIDERATION

Sometimes it takes a neutral third person to assist people in uncovering and appreciating their common ground.

FIRST STEPS

To develop common ground with others:

1. Have a real desire to come to terms about a difference.
2. Ask the other person to tell his side of the story without interrupting.
3. Identify the issues involved; for example:
   - Some specific bit of information
   - How to get something done
   - What the end result is supposed to be and why
   - How people communicate with each other
   - Underlying values, beliefs, or assumptions related to individual diversity
4. Ask the other person to describe her interests, needs, and wants.
5. Share your own interests, needs, and wants.
6. Brainstorm options to meet each of your expressed interests.
7. Make an agreement that clearly describes who will do what by when.

REFLECTION

Recall a recent disagreement you had with someone at work. What was at stake for you? For the other person? Was there any common ground? What factors helped or hindered reaching an agreement?

NEXT STEP

Describe an issue you currently have with someone at work. What may be the possible misunderstandings underlying that issue?

SESSION SYNTHESIS

- What insights or new awareness did you gain in this session?
- What key learnings are associated with those insights?
- Which Coaching Points or aspects were easier to work through?
- Which Coaching Points or aspects were more difficult to work through?
- What specific steps or actions have you already taken? What occurred or didn't occur?
- What specific steps or actions do you feel most resistant to taking? What is underlying that resistance?
- What questions or concerns remain unanswered for you right now? What are you going to do about it?

COACHING SESSION FOUR

■

Expressing Yourself Assertively

In this session you will explore the following Coaching Points:

- ASSERTIVENESS
- FEEDBACK
- NETWORKING
- PRESENTATION
- WORK

Now that you have examined (1) how behavior affects interpersonal interaction, (2) the essential components of effective communication, and (3) the challenges of dealing with differences and conflict, you are ready to integrate your learning in order to constructively and effectively express yourself with others.

Getting along with others involves developing the ability and skill to clearly and confidently communicate in a manner that is heard and acknowledged by others. Once again, people will have different perspectives or points of view, so you will always be faced with the challenge of communicating in a way that will be understood by others. Though your point of view may not be accepted outright, your ability to engage others with mutual respect and the willingness to explore any differences openly and honestly will go a long way toward achieving common goals.

The first two Coaching Points you will explore in this session concern how to express your thoughts, opinions, and feelings assertively and give clear feedback to others about your perceptions.

From there, the next areas for you to explore are concerned with developing the ability to network with colleagues and the skill to present information in a manner that supports and enhances a collaborative work environment.

ASSERTIVENESS is being *direct* and *honest* in the way you communicate your needs and wants to others.

SIMPLE TRUTH

Ask for what you want—you have a better chance of getting it than if you don't ask.

FOR YOUR CONSIDERATION

Set limits on your time and energy by saying no when appropriate.

FIRST STEPS

To assert yourself in a positive manner:

1. Assess what is at stake for you in a particular situation.
2. Reflect on your thoughts and feelings about the people involved and the environment you are all in.
3. Express your honest feelings without hurting another's feelings or placing blame on them.
4. Exercise your personal rights without denying the rights of others.
5. Negotiate with others to create a mutually winning situation with no loser.

REFLECTION

Consider a person you work with. What would you like to say to her or him? What would you rather not say to her or him? Why?

NEXT STEP

Outline what you can do and say to assert yourself the next time you interact with that person.

FEEDBACK is the information you give another person about your *perceptions* of that person's *behavior* or *performance*.

> **SIMPLE TRUTH**
>
> *Feedback often says as much about the person giving it as the person receiving it.*

FOR YOUR CONSIDERATION

Feedback should not attack or place blame on someone else; instead it should present an opportunity for exploring assumptions and learning from mistakes.

FIRST STEPS

Before you give someone feedback, consider the following:

1. What is your emotional state? (Are you tired? Do you have personal problems? Are you feeling pressured?)
2. What are your feelings toward the person? (Do you like the person?)
3. What are your feelings about the feedback you want to give? (Are you comfortable or uncomfortable with it?)
4. Is the time and place for providing the feedback appropriate?

Then, to provide constructive feedback to someone:

1. Ask the person's permission to offer him or her some feedback.
   "I've been thinking about how our project's been going. Can we talk about it?"
2. Share your perceptions about what you've observed in a clear and direct manner.
   "I think that the calculations in the report are incorrect. Is there anything that may have distracted you today?
3. Initiate a conversation by asking the person about his or her perspective in an open-ended and supportive manner.

REFLECTION

Recall when someone gave you feedback on your behavior or performance. How did you receive it? Why was the feedback effective or ineffective?

NEXT STEP

Consider a co-worker to whom you want to give feedback. Prepare for giving that feedback, then set a time and place to offer it.

NETWORKING is developing *informal relationships* with other people to connect, share, and gain support for your separate or mutual goals.

> **SIMPLE TRUTH**
>
> *Give more than you expect to receive and appreciate that timing can be everything.*

FOR YOUR CONSIDERATION

Creating a supportive network involves letting others know how important they are to you and being assertive, not aggressive, when seeking and sharing information.

FIRST STEPS

1. Collect and share information, sources of information, or referrals to other people or situations with those you already know or may want to get to know.
2. Volunteer to serve on company-wide, interdepartmental, or departmental task forces and committees.
3. Participate in celebrations and social occasions within your organization.
4. Become involved in community, business, industry, educational, and professional groups that share your interests.

REFLECTION

What is your initial reaction to meeting someone new? Do you prefer to approach the new person, be approached, or be introduced by a third person?

NEXT STEP

Describe the information you have that could be of support to someone else. What information might you need from others? Make a list of people who you could network with and the information you could offer them or ask them for.

PRESENTATION is communicating with the intent to influence people to think or do something differently.

> SIMPLE TRUTH
>
> *People are usually interested in what's in it for them.*

FOR YOUR CONSIDERATION

To appeal to people's minds, present clear logic and facts; to appeal to people's hearts, present anecdotes and stories.

FIRST STEPS

When preparing a presentation:

1. Determine what you most want to achieve:
   - Offer a report.
   - Persuade others to your point of view.
2. Identify the audience you need to address:
   - Is it one person or a group of people?
   - How much time will you have to capture their attention?
   - Is their style formal or informal?
3. Include the following components:
   - An overview that describes the purpose of the communication
   - The substance that explains your point of view, the issue, reasons why it is important, and its benefits or consequences for them
   - A summary, conclusion, and suggestions for any action you want them to take.
4. Determine whether the presentation should be delivered in written form, oral form, or both, depending on the nature of the content and the need for personal contact.

REFLECTION

Find a memo you recently received. What is it about its style and format that made you want to read it, or not? Recall a presentation you attended. What about the presenter's vocal style, gestures, and attitude either made you want to listen closely or tune out?

NEXT STEP

Who do you need to influence about what at work? Outline a presentation of the main points you need to make.

WORK is a process of *communicating* and *interacting* with others to address common problems or accomplish common objectives or goals.

SIMPLE TRUTH

Working at high performance is not a solo activity.

FOR YOUR CONSIDERATION

Within your company or work group you have both a "supplier" for what you need in order to do your work and, in turn, you have a "customer" for what you supply.

FIRST STEPS

To develop productive working relationships:

1. Determine who your current and potential *customers* and *suppliers* are.
2. Find out what your customers need and when they need it.
3. Identify the people and resources available or needed to get the work done effectively and efficiently.
4. Establish guidelines for working together.
5. Address your assumptions, interaction styles, and power and privilege dynamics.
6. Determine measurements for evaluating productivity and success.
7. Continually learn by planning, acting, observing results, and reflecting on ways to make improvements.

REFLECTION

When was the last time you discussed your mutual needs with your customers and suppliers? What prevents you from keeping up to date with them? In what ways do you compete for resources? In what ways do you share success?

NEXT STEP

Outline what you can do to better accomplish common work goals with others.

SESSION SYNTHESIS

- What insights or new awareness did you gain in this session?
- What key learnings are associated with those insights?
- Which Coaching Points or aspects were easier to work through?
- Which Coaching Points or aspects were more difficult to work through?
- What specific steps or actions have you already taken? What occurred or didn't occur?
- What specific steps or actions do you feel most resistant to taking? What is underlying that resistance?
- What questions or concerns remain unanswered for you right now? What are you going to do about it?

ABOUT THE AUTHOR

MICHAEL BAROFF has 20 years experience collaborating with organizations to achieve business strategy and change management outcomes, work process improvement, and human resource performance results. He applies a unique blend of competencies in the areas of qualitative research, work systems analysis, information synthesis, process intervention and training design, facilitation, dialogue, mediation, and coaching.

He has consulted to numerous companies in a wide range of industries, government agencies, nonprofit organizations, educational institutions, and community groups, including the Internal Revenue Service, Metropolitan Water District, Jet Propulsion Laboratory, Consumer Credit Counseling Service, Prudential Insurance, PacifiCare Health Systems, Nissan Motor Corporation, Federal Express, Xerox Corporation, Blue Cross, Southern California Gas Company, University of California, Armstrong World Industries, Amway, United Way, and the Los Angeles Unified School District.

Baroff is former president of the Los Angeles Chapter of the American Society for Training and Development (ASTD). He has contributed articles on workplace performance improvement topics to the *Society for the Advancement of Management Newsletter*, *Supervisor's Guide to Quality and Excellence*, ASTD *Interchange*, and *The Tao of Dialogue: A Manual of Dialogic Communication*. He has spoken and conducted workshops at conferences and association meetings for ASTD, Center for Nonprofit Management, the State of California Office of Continuous Improvement, the Personnel Testing Council, and the International Society for Performance Improvement. He conducts customized workshops to assist organizations in introducing and integrating the *Inner Work of Work* guidebook material.

The author would appreciate learning about your experiences using this guidebook. Please send your feedback and comments to him via mail, e-mail, or the *Inner Work of Work* Web site.

Michael Baroff
Organization Effectiveness Consulting
2461 Santa Monica Blvd., PMB 337
Santa Monica, CA 90404
(310) 285-8043
Mbaroff@aol.com
http://www.innerworkcoaching.com

ORDER THE INNER WORK OF WORK SERIES

Four ways to order:

- **ONLINE** 24 hours a day through our secure server: bkconnection.com
- **CALL TOLL-FREE** 7 A.M. to 12 midnight: 800-929-2929
- **FAX** to 802-864-762
- **MAIL** to Berrett-Koehler Communications, PO Box 565, Williston, VT 05495

EACH GUIDEBOOK IS $10.95

BUY ALL THREE AND SAVE 10% FOR A TOTAL OF $29.50

PLEASE USE THE FOLLOWING IDENTIFICATION NUMBERS WHEN ORDERING:

Being Your Best	ISBN 1-58376-153-5	Item #61535-705
Getting Along With Others	ISBN 1-58376-154-3	Item #61543-705
Contributing to Your Company's Success	ISBN 1-58376-155-1	Item #61551-705
Set of all three	ISBN 1-58376-152-7	Item #61535-705

ORDER IN QUANTITY AND SAVE!

10–49: $9.85 (per unit)
500–999: $7.66
50–99: $9.30
1000–1999: $7.11
100–499: $8.21
2000–2999: $6.57

Call Berrett-Koehler Special Sales for information at 415-288-0260.

BK

Berrett-Koehler Communications, Inc.

450 Sansome Street, Suite 1200, San Francisco, CA 94111

COACHING PROMPTS

As you work through each Coaching Point, you may want to keep this insert at hand so you can refer to the prompts below.

DEFINITION

Coaching Prompt: As you read the Definition, what stands out for you? Note your immediate responses. Do you agree or disagree with this Definition? Does it make you think of any experiences at work?

SIMPLE TRUTH

Coaching Prompt: Does the Simple Truth ring true? If so, describe an experience that makes it real for you. If not, note what situation in your experience suggests something different.

FOR YOUR CONSIDERATION

Coaching Prompt: Think about the practical implications and consequences of the For Your Consideration statement. What experiences, if any, have you had that confirm this statement? Have you had any experiences that suggest this statement isn't always true? Keep in mind that all of the statements within the Coaching Points are only guides; it is your experience that counts.

FIRST STEPS

Coaching Prompt: Read through each of the First Steps and make notes to yourself in response to each question or suggestion.

REFLECTION

Coaching Prompt: Remember that reflection happens best when you are in an open and relaxed state of mind. Sometimes it is hard to make this happen. It can help to take a deep breath and close your eyes for a moment before you begin. Then, read the statement and take some time to look within yourself and consider what meaning it has for you.

NEXT STEP

Coaching Prompt: You should now be ready to outline some Next Steps. Be very specific for each action. Make an agreement with yourself about when, where, and with whom these actions will take place.

Appreciate and acknowledge your progress no matter what pace you move at in your journey. —MICHAEL BAROFF